WORKBOOK:

LIFEPASS

A GUIDE TO DROP YOUR LIMITS AND RISE TO YOUR POTENTIAL.

The Copyright of this book
belongs to Great Creative.

It should not be remade or
reproduced without the
permission of the Writer.

DEDICATION

To You, My Reader

This is a **SEVEN STEP GUIDE TO DROP YOUR LIMITS AND RISE TO YOUR POTENTIAL.**

INSTRUCTIONS

1. HAVE A PEN/PENCIL WITH YOU AS YOU STUDY THIS WORKBOOK
2. IN THE "NOTES" SECTION, WRITE DOWN THE THOUGHTS THAT RAN THROUGH YOUR HEAD WHILE NAVIGATING EACH STEP
3. PRACTICE ALL YOU LEARN FROM THIS WORKBOOK.

NAME:

_____

_____

AGE:

_____

OCCUPATION:

_____

_____

_____

RELATIONSHIP STATUS:

_____

_____

In this workbook, which is in line with PayPal Kadakia's well-written book, Great Creative offers an effective practical approach to meet up with everything that has been outlined in there and more!

It seems nearly impossible to rise to our potential with so many limitations. Great Creative provides applicable ways of dropping your limits and reaching your full potential.

This is a book that you cannot afford to miss as it is of great value!

STEP 1

"EMBRACE UNCOMFORTABLE SITUATIONS."

First, of the things you can do to reach your full potential is a tip that you will least want to come to terms with. Embracing uncomfortable situations and breaking out of your comfort zone is never an easy task. One of the main reasons that people aren't achieving their highest potential for success is because they are scared, uncomfortable, or anxious to take the first steps.

Decisions like these will allow you to see how big of an opportunity you can open for yourself if you embrace being uncomfortable.

TASK

Once in a while, do things that will take you out of your comfort zone.

TIPS

Most times, uncomfortable situations don't remain uncomfortable forever. It only takes a matter of time.

NOTES

STEP 2

"BE A CONSISTENT GOAL MAKER."

People who are successful set goals. Being a consistent goal maker will allow you to set goals to live a better life that will push you outside of your comfort zone and toward your full potential.

Taking the big picture of your life and incorporating goals into each step of the way will allow you to move toward them on a daily basis, rather than waiting until you are "ready." Being consistent with your goal making will also help you to focus on the goals at hand, no matter how small they may be. It will condition you into achieving even the highest of goals.

TASK

Set up long term and short term goals for yourself.

TIPS

You are never truly ready for the next stage in your life, you simply have to take the plunge.

NOTES

_____

_____

_____

_____

_____

_____

_____

_____

_____

_____

_____

_____

_____

_____

_____

_____

_____

_____

STEP 3

"TAKE ACTION EACH DAY."

Having an unsatisfying daily routine will never amount to success. Being able to take action toward your goals each day will provide you with a routine of stepping outside of your comfort zone until it becomes a norm.

Being able to reach your full potential does not leave room for boring and comfortable days in which you take zero action to improve.

TASK

Make plans on how to work towards your goals and take action!

TIPS

Think of each day as an opportunity to reach your goals. Doing things that are out of the ordinary will help you to turn this action into a habit.

NOTES

STEP 4

"PUT YOURSELF IN LEARNING SITUATIONS."

Put yourself in situations you will constantly learn from. Don't allow your brain to become stagnant. Instead, you should practice consistently putting yourself in situations that you can learn from.

A successful person who will reach their full potential knows that along the way they have to surround themselves with people and resources that will provide consistent knowledge.

TASK

Live by this Confucious quote:

"If you are the smartest person in the room, then you are in the wrong room."

TIPS

As one of the best things you can do to reach your full potential, learning from others and learning from yourself are two of the most important ways to succeed.

NOTES

STEP 5

"LEARN FROM YOUR PAST."

Learning from your past and being stuck in the past are two entirely different approaches to deciphering your past decisions. When you think of your past, you should also consider your present and future.

You will also be able to face your responsibilities and discover what you are truly capable of during this process.

TASK

Consider your past by asking, "What are my strengths?" rather than being overwhelmed by your downfalls.

TIPS

A person who does not allow their past to weigh them down, and rather uses their past to motivate and provide for their future, is a successful one.

NOTES

_____

_____

_____

_____

_____

_____

_____

_____

_____

_____

_____

_____

_____

_____

_____

_____

_____

_____

_____

_____

STEP 6

"BECOME ACCOUNTABLE FOR YOUR ACTIONS."

Becoming accountable for your actions is one of the best things you can do to rise to your full potential. Being able to look at yourself in the mirror and take responsibility for your actions when necessary is not only a great practice of being humble but something that will allow you to pinpoint your past mistakes.

TASK

Take a step back and focus on the decisions that led you to a negative outcome. This will encourage you to examine your behavior and better understand your path, and how you will move forward.

<u>TIPS</u>

Instead of constantly blaming someone else, or thinking the world is against you, you will provide yourself with a chance to improve and learn by taking responsibility.

NOTES

STEP 7

"SAY GOODBYE TO STRESS AND NEGATIVITY."

When you think of yourself achieving your full potential, do you think of this person being stressed and negative? We hope not. If you picture yourself as a better and more successful person in the future, why not start to feel like them now? Or at least pretend to feel like your potential self; fake it until you make it.

Better said than done, letting go
of stress and negativity is a huge
task in itself.

TASK

Always try to see the bright side
of things and remain hopeful.

TIPS

One of the best things you can do
to reach your full potential,
maintaining an optimistic
mindset will improve your life
drastically, opening opportunities
for success.

NOTES

WE HAVE SUCCESSFULLY COME TO THE END OF THIS WORKBOOK.

AFTER FOLLOWING THE ABOVE STATED STEPS, EVALUATE YOURSELF AND REPEAT THE SAME STEPS!

HOW HAS THIS WORKBOOK HELPED YOU?

_____

_____

_____

_____

_____

_____

_____

_____

_____

_____

_____

_____

_____

_____

_____

_____

PERSONAL NOTES

_____

_____

_____

_____

_____

_____

_____

_____

_____

_____

_____

_____

_____

_____

_____

_____

_____

_____

_____

OTHER THINGS

CPSIA information can be obtained
at www.ICGtesting.com
Printed in the USA
LVHW082143310522
720184LV00022B/515